HAL•LEONARD

JAZZ PLAY-ALONG®

Book and CD for B♭, E♭, C and Bass Clef Instruments

volume
161

dav
brubeck

T0071688

Arranged and
Produced by
Mark Taylor

BOOK

TITLE	PAGE NUMBERS			
	C Treble Instruments	B♭ Instruments	E♭ Instruments	C Bass Instruments
Blue Rondo a la Turk	7	29	51	73
Brandenburg Gate	10	32	54	76
The Duke	12	34	56	78
Golden Horn	14	36	58	80
In Your Own Sweet Way	16	38	60	82
It's a Raggy Waltz	18	40	62	84
Marble Arch	20	42	64	86
Take Five	22	44	66	88
Thank You (Dziekuje)	24	46	68	90
The Trolley Song	4	26	48	70

CD

TITLE	CD Track Number Split Track/Melody	CD Track Number Full Stereo Track
Blue Rondo a la Turk	1	2
Brandenburg Gate	3	4
The Duke	5	6
Golden Horn	7	8
In Your Own Sweet Way	9	10
It's a Raggy Waltz	11	12
Marble Arch	13	14
Take Five	15	16
Thank You (Dziekuje)	17	18
The Trolley Song	19	20
B♭ Tuning Notes		21

Photo by William "PoPsie" Randolph
www.PoPsiePhotos.com

ISBN 978-1-4584-0755-9

Music Sales America

EXCLUSIVELY DISTRIBUTED BY

HAL•LEONARD®
CORPORATION
7777 W. BLUEMOUND RD. P.O. BOX 13819 MILWAUKEE, WI 53213

Visit Hal Leonard Online at
www.halleonard.com

DAVE BRUBECK

Volume 161

Arranged and Produced by
Mark Taylor

Featured Players:

Graham Breedlove–Trumpet
John Desalme–Tenor Sax
Tony Nalker–Piano
Jim Roberts–Bass/Guitar
Todd Harrison–Drums

**Recorded at Bias Studios, Springfield, Virginia
Bob Dawson, Engineer**

HOW TO USE THE CD:

Each song has <u>two</u> tracks:

1) Split Track/Melody

Woodwind, Brass, Keyboard, and **Mallet Players** can use this track as a learning tool for melody style and inflection.

Bass Players can learn and perform with this track – remove the recorded bass track by turning down the volume on the LEFT channel.

Keyboard and **Guitar Players** can learn and perform with this track – remove the recorded piano part by turning down the volume on the RIGHT channel.

2) Full Stereo Track

Soloists or **Groups** can learn and perform with this accompaniment track with the RHYTHM SECTION only.

THE TROLLEY SONG

WORDS AND MUSIC BY HUGH MARTIN
AND RALPH BLANE

D.S. AL FINE
TAKE REPEAT

BLUE RONDO A LA TURK

BY DAVE BRUBECK

C VERSION

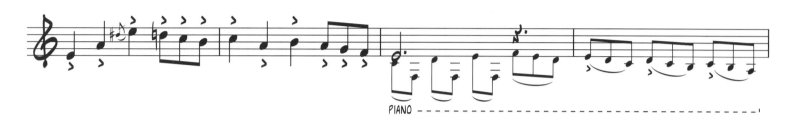

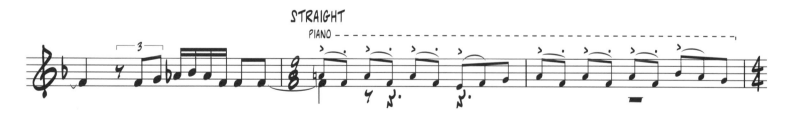

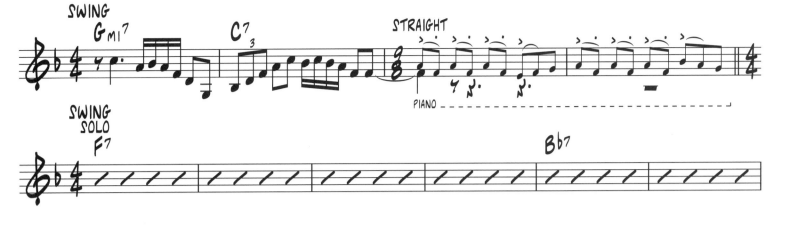

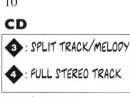

BRANDENBURG GATE

BY DAVE BRUBECK

C VERSION

SOLO (2 CHORUSES)

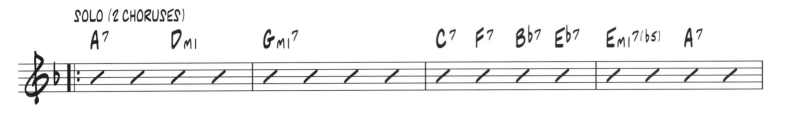

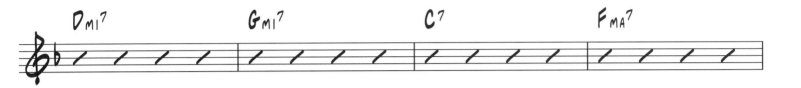

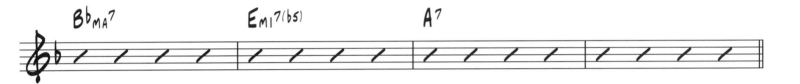

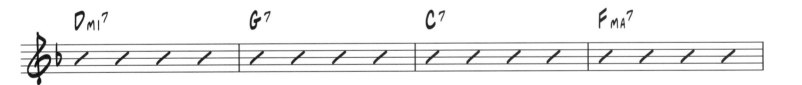

D.S. AL CODA

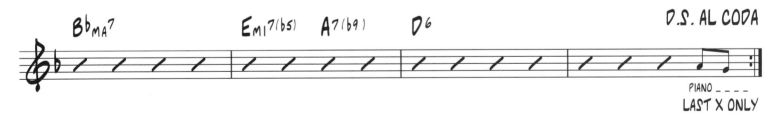

PIANO _ _ _ _
LAST X ONLY

CODA

THE DUKE

BY DAVE BRUBECK

GOLDEN HORN

BY DAVE BRUBECK

C VERSION

FAST LATIN

D.S. AL CODA
TAKE REPEAT

CD
9 : SPLIT TRACK/MELODY
10 : FULL STEREO TRACK

IN YOUR OWN SWEET WAY

BY DAVE BRUBECK

C VERSION

MEDIUM LIGHT SWING

Bb MA7 Eb MA7   Ab mi7 Db7   Gb MA7 B MA7   F+7(#9) B7   Bb7   Eb6

A mi7(b5) D7   G mi7 C7   C mi7 F7   Bb MA7 Eb MA7   Ab mi7 Db7

Gb MA7 B MA7 F+7(#9) B7   Bb7 Eb6   E mi7 A7   D MA7   E mi7 A7

D MA7   D mi7 G7 /F E mi7 Eb7   D mi7(b5) Ab7   G7   C mi7/Bb

A mi7(b5) D7   G mi7 C7   C mi7 F7   Bb MA7 Eb MA7   Ab mi7 Db7

D.S. AL CODA
TAKE REPEAT

Gb MA7 B MA7 F+7(#9) B7   Bb7   Eb mi7 Eb mi6   Eb mi(#5) Eb mi

2ND X ONLY

CODA Bb7   Bb+7(b9)   Eb mi   F/Eb

E7/Eb   Eb7   Ab mi/Eb

Bb7   A7 Ab7   G+7(#9) Gb MA7 F7(b5) E MA7(b5) Eb mi7

RIT.

IT'S A RAGGY WALTZ

BY DAVE BRUBECK

CD
- ♦11 : SPLIT TRACK/MELODY
- ♦12 : FULL STEREO TRACK

C VERSION

MEDIUM JAZZ WALTZ

TO CODA ⊕

SOLOS (2 CHORUSES)

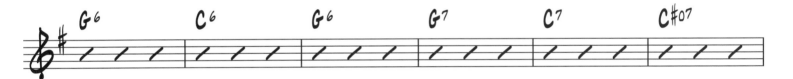

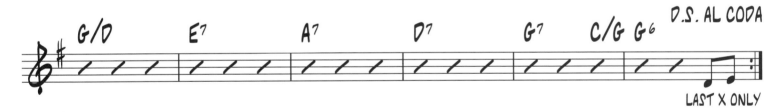

MARBLE ARCH

BY DAVE BRUBECK

C VERSION

TAKE FIVE

BY PAUL DESMOND

C VERSION

MEDIUM SWING

RHYTHM

TO CODA ⊕

CD

17 : SPLIT TRACK/MELODY
18 : FULL STEREO TRACK

C VERSION

THANK YOU
(DZIEKUJE)

BY DAVE BRUBECK

25

THE TROLLEY SONG

WORDS AND MUSIC BY HUGH MARTIN
AND RALPH BLANE

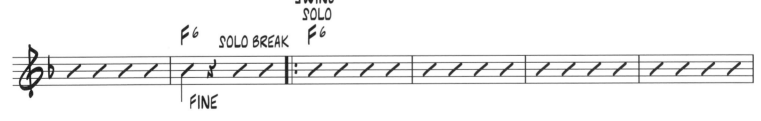
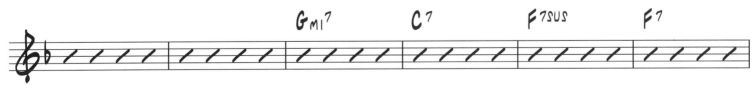

G_{MI}7   C7   F6   D_{MI}7   G_{MI}7   C7

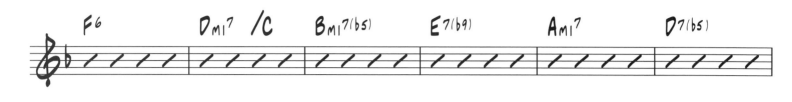

F6   D_{MI}7 /C   B_{MI}7(b5)   E7(b9)   A_{MI}7   D7(b5)

G#_{MI}7   C#7(b9)   G_{MI}7   C7(b9)   F6

G_{MI}7   C7

F7SUS   F7   Bb6   Bb_{MI}6   F6/A

Bb07   F6/C   Bb_{MI}6/C#   D_{MI}7(b5)

G7(b9)   A_{MI}7(b5)   D7(b9)

G_{MI}7   A_{MI}7   Bb_{MA}7   A7(b9)

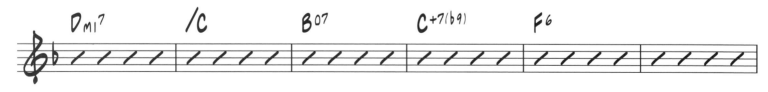

D_{MI}7   /C   B07   C+7(b9)   F6

D.S. AL FINE
TAKE REPEAT

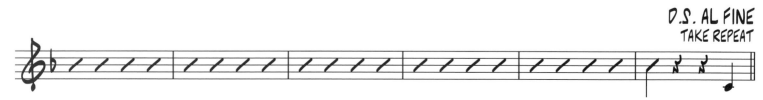

BLUE RONDO A LA TURK

BY DAVE BRUBECK

CD
1 : SPLIT TRACK/MELODY
2 : FULL STEREO TRACK

Bb VERSION

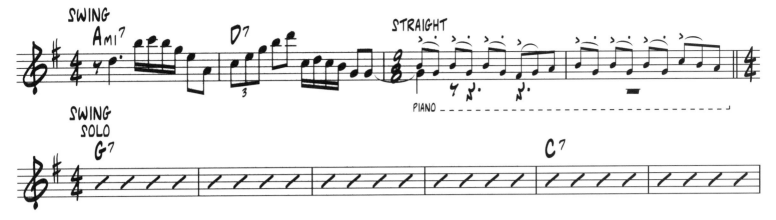
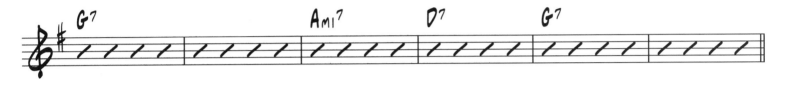

BRANDENBURG GATE

BY DAVE BRUBECK

Bb VERSION

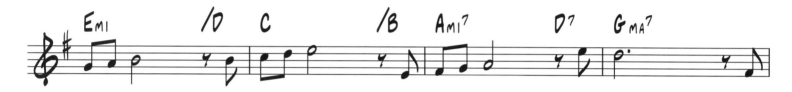

SOLO (2 CHORUSES)

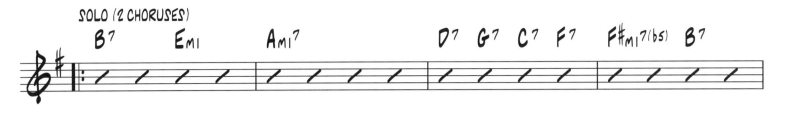

THE DUKE

BY DAVE BRUBECK

CD
◆ 5 : SPLIT TRACK/MELODY
◆ 6 : FULL STEREO TRACK

Bb VERSION

CD

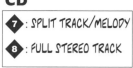

7 : SPLIT TRACK/MELODY
8 : FULL STEREO TRACK

GOLDEN HORN

BY DAVE BRUBECK

Bb VERSION

FAST LATIN

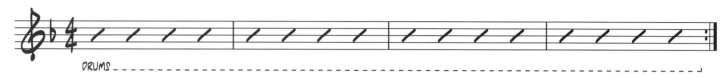

DRUMS -

(LATIN)

TO CODA

SOLO BREAK

SWING
SOLOS (4 CHORUSES)

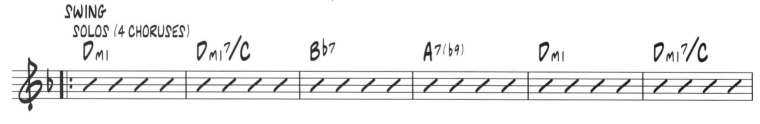

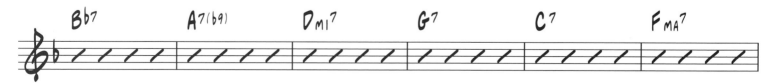

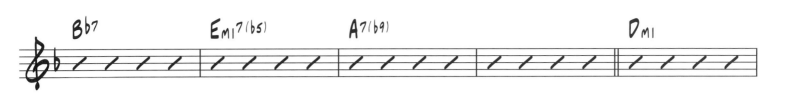

Bb7   Emi7(b5)   A7(b9)   Dmi

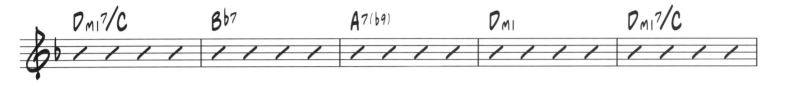

Dmi7/C   Bb7   A7(b9)   Dmi   Dmi7/C

Bb7   A7(b9)   Dmi7   G7   C7

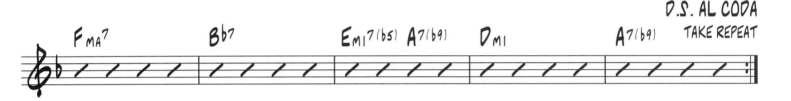

D.S. AL CODA
TAKE REPEAT

Fma7   Bb7   Emi7(b5) A7(b9)   Dmi   A7(b9)

CODA
Bb7   Emi7(b5)   A7(b9)   Dmi

DRUMS

Bb7   Emi7(b5)   A7(b9)   Dmi

DRUMS

C#7   Gmi7(b5)   C7(b9)   Fmi

DRUMS

Bb7   Emi7(b5)   A7(b9)   Dmi   N.C.

DRUMS

PIANO

CD

◆9 : SPLIT TRACK/MELODY
◆10 : FULL STEREO TRACK

IN YOUR OWN SWEET WAY

BY DAVE BRUBECK

Bb VERSION

MEDIUM LIGHT SWING

CD

IT'S A RAGGY WALTZ

BY DAVE BRUBECK

Bb VERSION

TO CODA ⊕

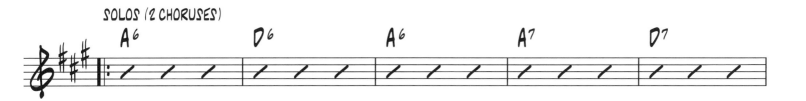

MARBLE ARCH

BY DAVE BRUBECK

CD
⑮ : SPLIT TRACK/MELODY
⑯ : FULL STEREO TRACK

TAKE FIVE

BY PAUL DESMOND

Bb VERSION

MEDIUM SWING

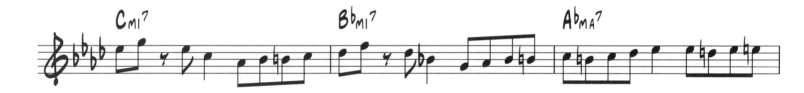

TO CODA ⊕

CD

17: SPLIT TRACK/MELODY
18: FULL STEREO TRACK

THANK YOU
(DZIEKUJE)

BY DAVE BRUBECK

Bb VERSION

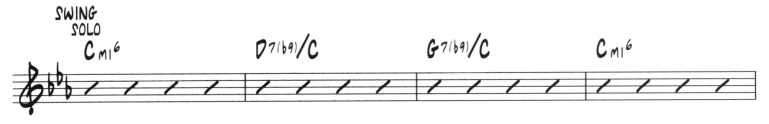

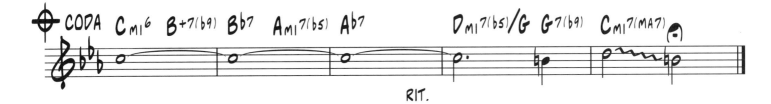

THE TROLLEY SONG

WORDS AND MUSIC BY HUGH MARTIN
AND RALPH BLANE

CD
19 : SPLIT TRACK/MELODY
20 : FULL STEREO TRACK

Eb VERSION

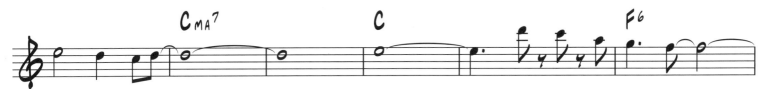

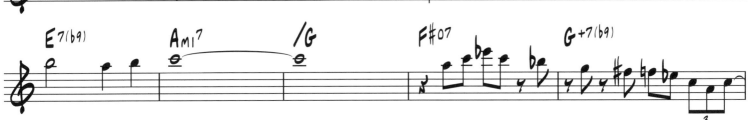

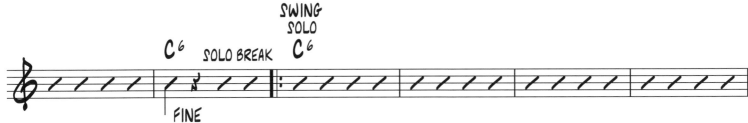
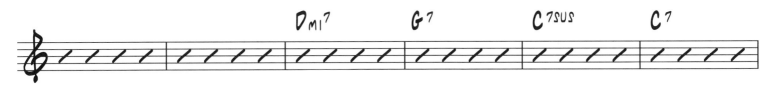

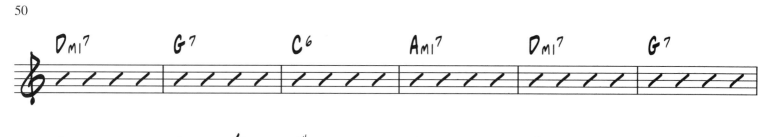

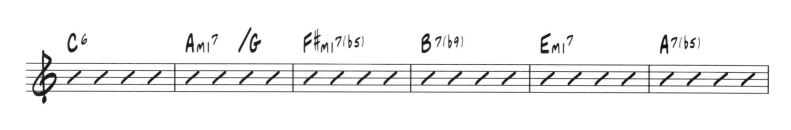

BLUE RONDO A LA TURK

BY DAVE BRUBECK

Eb VERSION

52

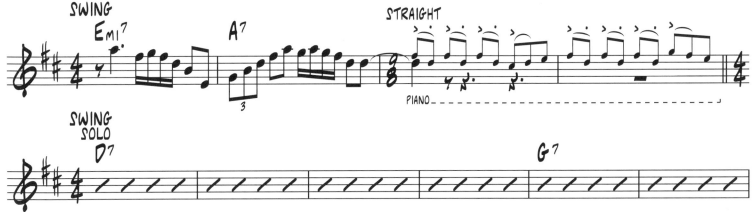

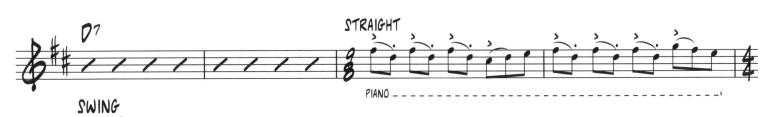

CD

◆3 : SPLIT TRACK/MELODY

◆4 : FULL STEREO TRACK

BRANDENBURG GATE

BY DAVE BRUBECK

Eb VERSION

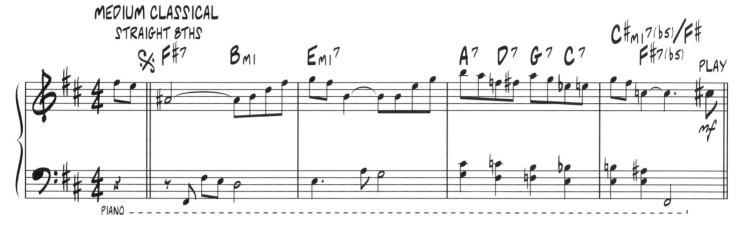

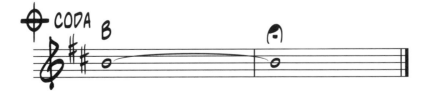

THE DUKE

BY DAVE BRUBECK

PIANO

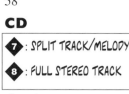

GOLDEN HORN

BY DAVE BRUBECK

Eb VERSION

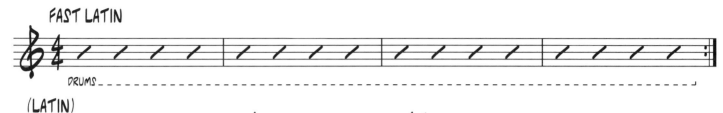

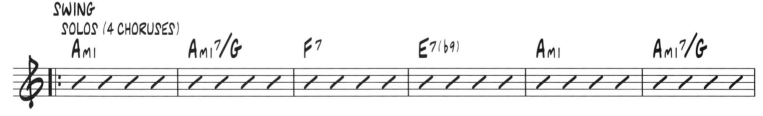

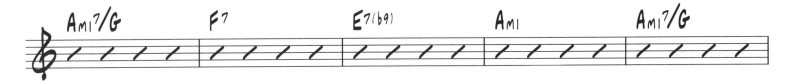

IN YOUR OWN SWEET WAY

BY DAVE BRUBECK

CD
9 : SPLIT TRACK/MELODY
10 : FULL STEREO TRACK

Eb VERSION

IT'S A RAGGY WALTZ

BY DAVE BRUBECK

Eb VERSION

MEDIUM JAZZ WALTZ

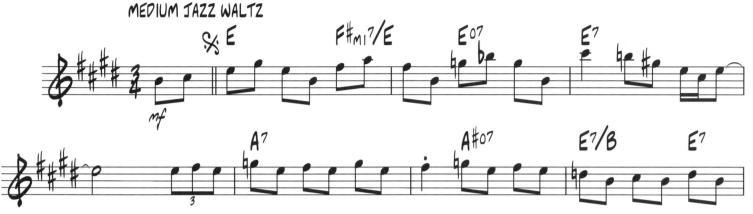

63

MARBLE ARCH

CD
◆13 : SPLIT TRACK/MELODY
◆14 : FULL STEREO TRACK

BY DAVE BRUBECK

Eb VERSION

CD

◆ 15 : SPLIT TRACK/MELODY
◆ 16 : FULL STEREO TRACK

TAKE FIVE

BY PAUL DESMOND

Eb VERSION

67

SOLO

D.S. AL CODA

CD

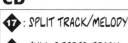

🔶17 : SPLIT TRACK/MELODY
🔶18 : FULL STEREO TRACK

THANK YOU
(DZIEKUJE)

BY DAVE BRUBECK

Eb VERSION

MEDIUM CLASSICAL
STRAIGHT 8THS

69

SWING
SOLO

Gmi6 | A7(b9)/G | D7(b9)/G | Gmi6 |

EbMA7 | D7(b9) | G7   G7(b9) | Cmi7   /Bb |

Ami7(b5) | D7(b9) | Gmi6 | D7/F# |

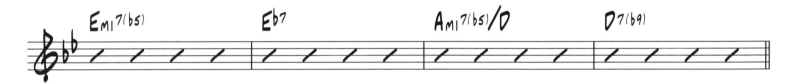

Emi7(b5) | Eb7 | Ami7(b5)/D | D7(b9) |

Gmi6 | A7(b9)/G | D7(b9)/G | Gmi6 |

EbMA7 | D7(b9) | G7   G7(b9) | Cmi7   /Bb |

Ami7(b5) | D7(b9) | Gmi6   D7(b9)/A | Bb6   G7(b9)/B |

D.S. AL CODA

Cmi7 | D+7 | Gmi6 | Ami7(b5)   D7(b9) |

CODA Gmi6   F#+7(b9)   F7   Emi7(b5)   Eb7 | Ami7(b5)/D   D7(b9)   Gmi7(MA7)

RIT.

THE TROLLEY SONG

WORDS AND MUSIC BY HUGH MARTIN
AND RALPH BLANE

F_{MI}^7 B^{b7} E^{b6} C_{MI}^7 F_{MI}^7 B^{b7}

E^{b6} C_{MI}^7 /B^b $A_{MI}^{7(b5)}$ $D^{7(b9)}$ G_{MI}^7 $C^{7(b5)}$

$F\#_{MI}^7$ $B^{7(b9)}$ F_{MI}^7 $B^{b7(b9)}$ E^{b6}

F_{MI}^7 B^{b7}

E^{b7SUS} E^{b7} A^{b6} $A^b_{MI}^6$ E^{b6}/G

A^{b07} E^{b6}/B^b $A^b_{MI}^6$/B $C_{MI}^{7(b5)}$

$F^{7(b9)}$ $G_{MI}^{7(b5)}$ $C^{7(b9)}$

F_{MI}^7 G_{MI}^7 $A^b_{MA}^7$ $G^{7(b9)}$

C_{MI}^7 /B^b A^{07} $B^{b+7(b9)}$ E^{b6}

D.S. AL FINE
TAKE REPEAT

CD

1 : SPLIT TRACK/MELODY
2 : FULL STEREO TRACK

BLUE RONDO A LA TURK

BY DAVE BRUBECK

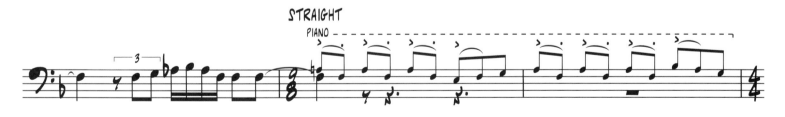

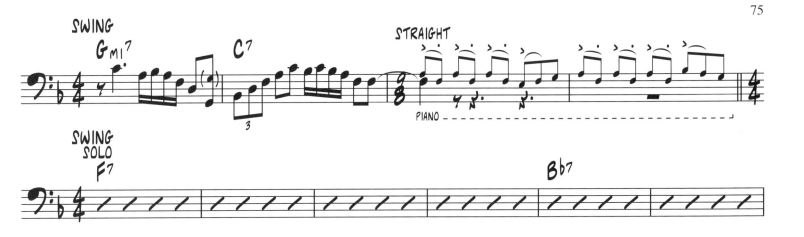

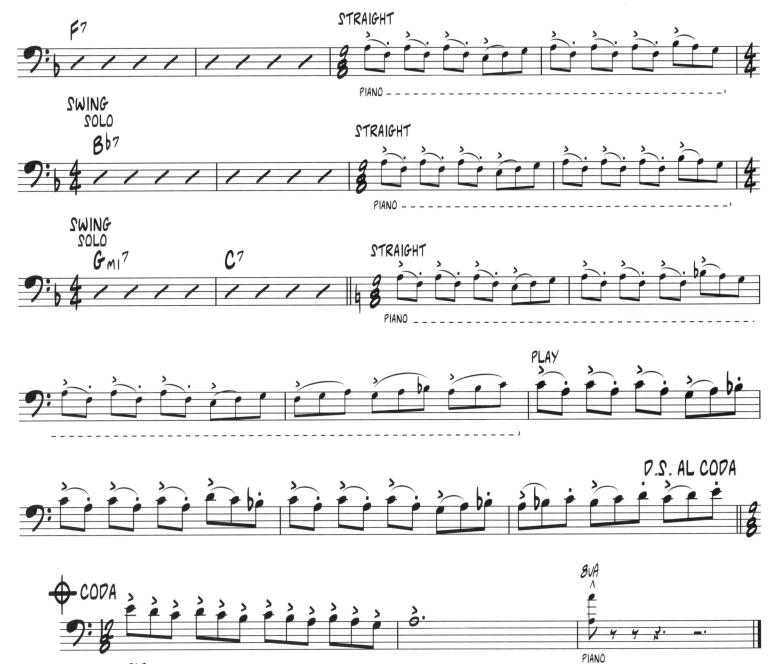

BRANDENBURG GATE

BY DAVE BRUBECK

𝄢: C VERSION

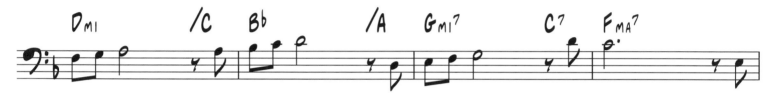

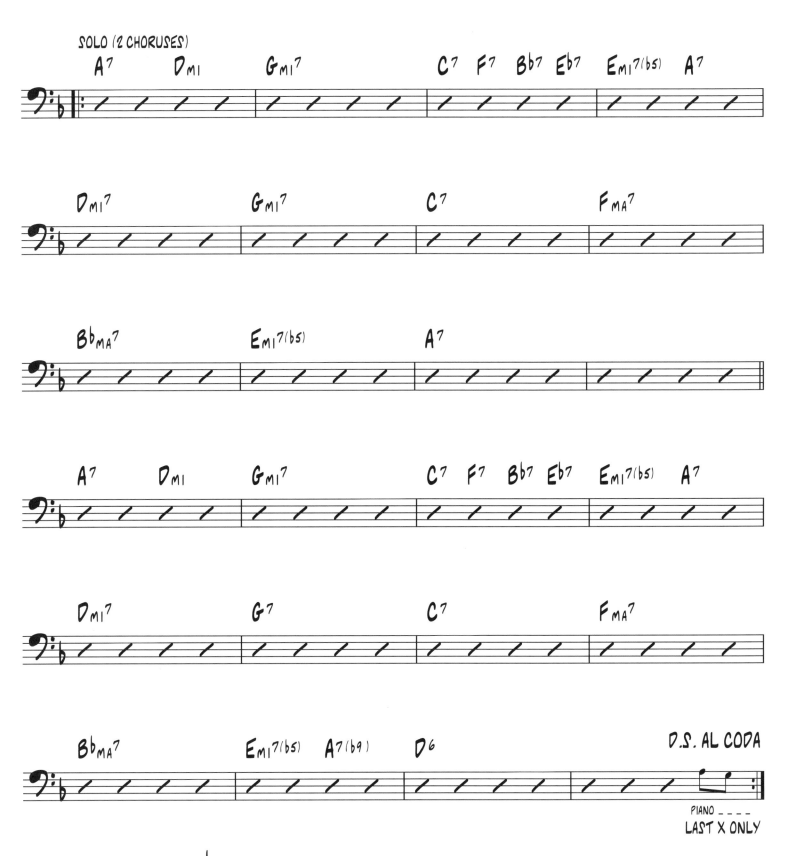

THE DUKE

BY DAVE BRUBECK

: SPLIT TRACK/MELODY
: FULL STEREO TRACK

GOLDEN HORN

BY DAVE BRUBECK

𝄢: C VERSION

FAST LATIN

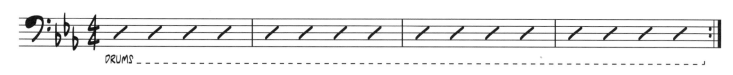

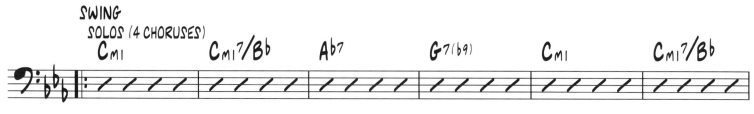

CD
9 : SPLIT TRACK/MELODY
10 : FULL STEREO TRACK

IN YOUR OWN SWEET WAY

BY DAVE BRUBECK

♪: C VERSION

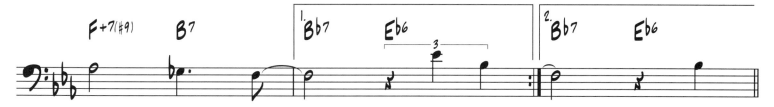

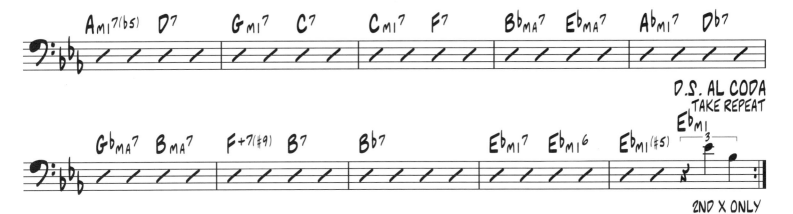

IT'S A RAGGY WALTZ

BY DAVE BRUBECK

CD

11 : SPLIT TRACK/MELODY

12 : FULL STEREO TRACK

𝄢 : C VERSION

MEDIUM JAZZ WALTZ

TO CODA ⊕

85

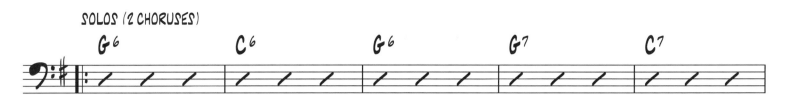

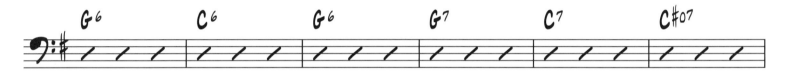

MARBLE ARCH

BY DAVE BRUBECK

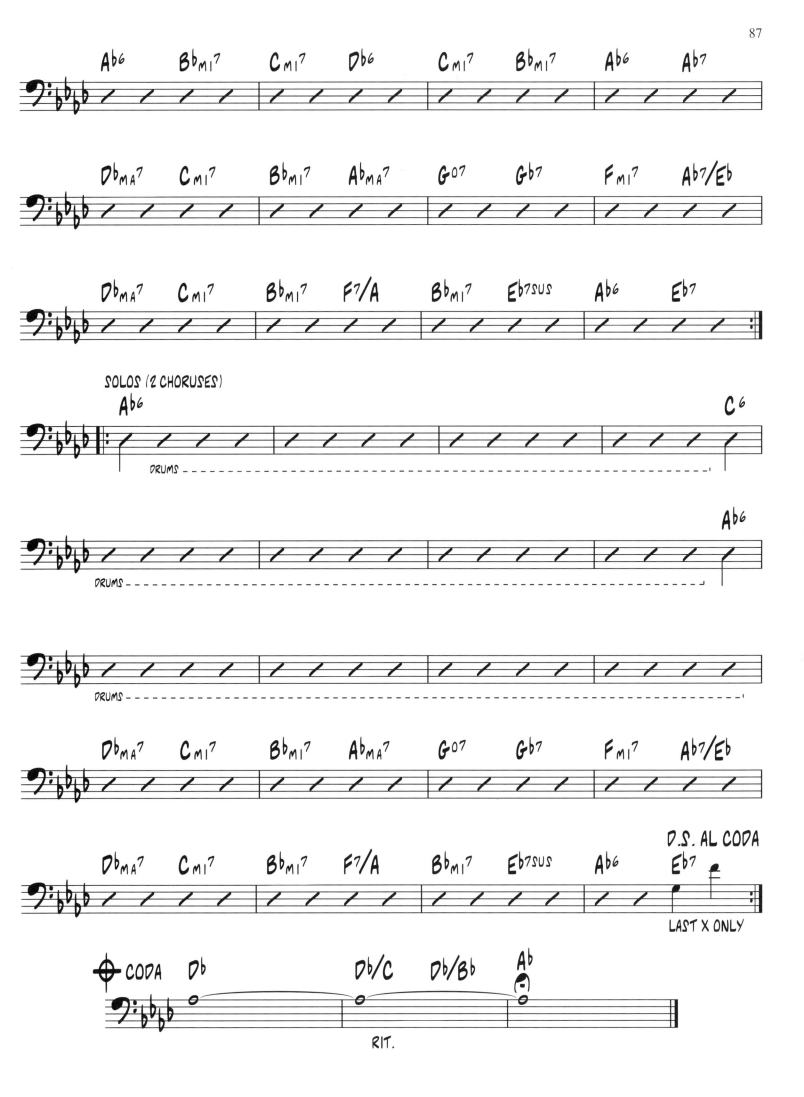

CD
15 : SPLIT TRACK/MELODY
16 : FULL STEREO TRACK

TAKE FIVE

BY PAUL DESMOND

𝄢: C VERSION

THANK YOU
(DZIEKUJE)

BY DAVE BRUBECK

SWING
SOLO

B♭mi6 · C7(♭9)/B♭ · F7(♭9)/B♭ · B♭mi6

G♭MA7 · F7(♭9) · B♭7 · B♭7(♭9) · E♭mi7 · /D♭

Cmi7(♭5) · F7(♭9) · B♭mi6 · F7/A

Gmi7(♭5) · G♭7 · Cmi7(♭5)/F · F7(♭9)

B♭mi6 · C7(♭9)/B♭ · F7(♭9)/B♭ · B♭mi6

G♭MA7 · F7(♭9) · B♭7 · B♭7(♭9) · E♭mi7 · /D♭

Cmi7(♭5) · F7(♭9) · B♭mi6 · F7(♭9)/C · D♭6 · B♭7(♭9)/D

D.S. AL CODA

E♭mi7 · F+7 · B♭mi6 · Cmi7(♭5) · F7(♭9)

CODA · B♭mi6 · A+7(♭9) · A♭7 · Gmi7(♭5) · G♭7 · Cmi7(♭5)/F · F7(♭9) · B♭mi7(MA7)

RIT.

Presenting the Hal Leonard JAZZ PLAY-ALONG SERIES

For use with all B-flat, E-flat, Bass Clef and C instruments, the Jazz Play-Along® Series is the ultimate learning tool for all jazz musicians. With musician-friendly lead sheets, melody cues, and other split-track choices on the included CD, these first-of-a-kind packages help you master improvisation while playing some of the greatest tunes of all time. FOR STUDY, each tune includes a split track with: melody cue with proper style and inflection • professional rhythm tracks • choruses for soloing • removable bass part • removable piano part. FOR PERFORMANCE, each tune also has: an additional full stereo accompaniment track (no melody) • additional choruses for soloing.

1A. MAIDEN VOYAGE/ALL BLUES
00843158 .... $15.99

1. DUKE ELLINGTON
00841644 .... $16.95

2. MILES DAVIS
00841645 .... $16.95

3. THE BLUES
00841646 .... $16.99

4. JAZZ BALLADS
00841691 .... $16.99

5. BEST OF BEBOP
00841689 .... $16.95

6. JAZZ CLASSICS WITH EASY CHANGES
00841690 .... $16.99

7. ESSENTIAL JAZZ STANDARDS
00843000 .... $16.99

8. ANTONIO CARLOS JOBIM AND THE ART OF THE BOSSA NOVA
00843001 .... $16.95

9. DIZZY GILLESPIE
00843002 .... $16.99

10. DISNEY CLASSICS
00843003 .... $16.99

11. RODGERS AND HART FAVORITES
00843004 .... $16.99

12. ESSENTIAL JAZZ CLASSICS
00843005 .... $16.99

13. JOHN COLTRANE
00843006 .... $16.95

14. IRVING BERLIN
00843007 .... $15.99

15. RODGERS & HAMMERSTEIN
00843008 .... $15.99

16. COLE PORTER
00843009 .... $15.95

17. COUNT BASIE
00843010 .... $16.95

18. HAROLD ARLEN
00843011 .... $15.95

19. COOL JAZZ
00843012 .... $15.95

20. CHRISTMAS CAROLS
00843080 .... $14.95

21. RODGERS AND HART CLASSICS
00843014 .... $14.95

22. WAYNE SHORTER
00843015 .... $16.95

23. LATIN JAZZ
00843016 .... $16.95

24. EARLY JAZZ STANDARDS
00843017 .... $14.95

25. CHRISTMAS JAZZ
00843018 .... $16.95

26. CHARLIE PARKER
00843019 .... $16.95

27. GREAT JAZZ STANDARDS
00843020 .... $16.99

28. BIG BAND ERA
00843021 .... $15.99

29. LENNON AND MCCARTNEY
00843022 .... $16.95

30. BLUES' BEST
00843023 .... $15.99

31. JAZZ IN THREE
00843024 .... $15.99

32. BEST OF SWING
00843025 .... $15.99

33. SONNY ROLLINS
00843029 .... $15.95

34. ALL TIME STANDARDS
00843030 .... $15.99

35. BLUESY JAZZ
00843031 .... $16.99

36. HORACE SILVER
00843032 .... $16.99

37. BILL EVANS
00843033 .... $16.95

38. YULETIDE JAZZ
00843034 .... $16.95

39. "ALL THE THINGS YOU ARE" & MORE JEROME KERN SONGS
00843035 .... $15.99

40. BOSSA NOVA
00843036 .... $16.99

41. CLASSIC DUKE ELLINGTON
00843037 .... $16.99

42. GERRY MULLIGAN FAVORITES
00843038 .... $16.99

43. GERRY MULLIGAN CLASSICS
00843039 .... $16.99

44. OLIVER NELSON
00843040 .... $16.95

45. GEORGE GERSHWIN
00103643 .... $24.99

46. BROADWAY JAZZ STANDARDS
00843042 .... $15.99

47. CLASSIC JAZZ BALLADS
00843043 .... $15.99

48. BEBOP CLASSICS
00843044 .... $16.99

49. MILES DAVIS STANDARDS
00843045 .... $16.95

50. GREAT JAZZ CLASSICS
00843046 .... $15.99

51. UP-TEMPO JAZZ
00843047 .... $15.99

52. STEVIE WONDER
00843048 .... $16.99

53. RHYTHM CHANGES
00843049 .... $15.99

54. "MOONLIGHT IN VERMONT" AND OTHER GREAT STANDARDS
00843050 .... $15.99

55. BENNY GOLSON
00843052 .... $15.95

56. "GEORGIA ON MY MIND" & OTHER SONGS BY HOAGY CARMICHAEL
00843056 .... $15.99

57. VINCE GUARALDI
00843057 .... $16.99

58. MORE LENNON AND MCCARTNEY
00843059 .... $16.99

59. SOUL JAZZ
00843060 .... $16.99

60. DEXTER GORDON
00843061 .... $15.95

61. MONGO SANTAMARIA
00843062 .... $15.95

62. JAZZ-ROCK FUSION
00843063 .... $16.99

63. CLASSICAL JAZZ
00843064 .... $14.95

64. TV TUNES
00843065 .... $14.95

65. SMOOTH JAZZ
00843066 .... $16.99

66. **A CHARLIE BROWN CHRISTMAS**
00843067 .... $16.99

67. **CHICK COREA**
00843068 .... $15.95

68. **CHARLES MINGUS**
00843069 .... $16.95

69. **CLASSIC JAZZ**
00843071 .... $15.99

70. **THE DOORS**
00843072 .... $14.95

71. **COLE PORTER CLASSICS**
00843073 .... $14.95

72. **CLASSIC JAZZ BALLADS**
00843074 .... $15.99

73. **JAZZ/BLUES**
00843075 .... $14.95

74. **BEST JAZZ CLASSICS**
00843076 .... $15.99

75. **PAUL DESMOND**
00843077 .... $16.99

76. **BROADWAY JAZZ BALLADS**
00843078 .... $15.99

77. **JAZZ ON BROADWAY**
00843079 .... $15.99

78. **STEELY DAN**
00843070 .... $15.99

79. **MILES DAVIS CLASSICS**
00843081 .... $15.99

80. **JIMI HENDRIX**
00843083 .... $16.99

81. **FRANK SINATRA – CLASSICS**
00843084 .... $15.99

82. **FRANK SINATRA – STANDARDS**
00843085 .... $16.99

83. **ANDREW LLOYD WEBBER**
00843104 .... $14.95

84. **BOSSA NOVA CLASSICS**
00843105 .... $14.95

85. **MOTOWN HITS**
00843109 .... $14.95

86. **BENNY GOODMAN**
00843110 .... $15.99

87. **DIXIELAND**
00843111 .... $16.99

88. **DUKE ELLINGTON FAVORITES**
00843112 .... $14.95

89. **IRVING BERLIN FAVORITES**
00843113 .... $14.95

90. **THELONIOUS MONK CLASSICS**
00841262 .... $16.99

91. **THELONIOUS MONK FAVORITES**
00841263 .... $16.99

92. **LEONARD BERNSTEIN**
00450134 .... $15.99

93. **DISNEY FAVORITES**
00843142 .... $14.99

94. **RAY**
00843143 .... $14.99

95. **JAZZ AT THE LOUNGE**
00843144 .... $14.99

96. **LATIN JAZZ STANDARDS**
00843145 .... $15.99

97. **MAYBE I'M AMAZED***
00843148 .... $15.99

98. **DAVE FRISHBERG**
00843149 .... $15.99

99. **SWINGING STANDARDS**
00843150 .... $14.99

100. **LOUIS ARMSTRONG**
00740423 .... $16.99

101. **BUD POWELL**
00843152 .... $14.99

102. **JAZZ POP**
00843153 .... $15.99

103. **ON GREEN DOLPHIN STREET
& OTHER JAZZ CLASSICS**
00843154 .... $14.99

104. **ELTON JOHN**
00843155 .... $14.99

105. **SOULFUL JAZZ**
00843151 .... $15.99

106. **SLO' JAZZ**
00843117 .... $14.99

107. **MOTOWN CLASSICS**
00843116 .... $14.99

108. **JAZZ WALTZ**
00843159 .... $15.99

109. **OSCAR PETERSON**
00843160 .... $16.99

110. **JUST STANDARDS**
00843161 .... $15.99

111. **COOL CHRISTMAS**
00843162 .... $15.99

112. **PAQUITO D'RIVERA – LATIN JAZZ***
48020662 .... $16.99

113. **PAQUITO D'RIVERA – BRAZILIAN JAZZ***
48020663 .... $19.99

114. **MODERN JAZZ QUARTET FAVORITES**
00843163 .... $15.99

115. **THE SOUND OF MUSIC**
00843164 .... $15.99

116. **JACO PASTORIUS**
00843165 .... $15.99

117. **ANTONIO CARLOS JOBIM – MORE HITS**
00843166 .... $15.99

118. **BIG JAZZ STANDARDS COLLECTION**
00843167 .... $27.50

119. **JELLY ROLL MORTON**
00843168 .... $15.99

120. **J.S. BACH**
00843169 .... $15.99

121. **DJANGO REINHARDT**
00843170 .... $15.99

122. **PAUL SIMON**
00843182 .... $16.99

123. **BACHARACH & DAVID**
00843185 .... $15.99

124. **JAZZ-ROCK HORN HITS**
00843186 .... $15.99

126. **COUNT BASIE CLASSICS**
00843157 .... $15.99

127. **CHUCK MANGIONE**
00843188 .... $15.99

128. **VOCAL STANDARDS (LOW VOICE)**
00843189 .... $15.99

129. **VOCAL STANDARDS (HIGH VOICE)**
00843190 .... $15.99

130. **VOCAL JAZZ (LOW VOICE)**
00843191 .... $15.99

131. **VOCAL JAZZ (HIGH VOICE)**
00843192 .... $15.99

132. **STAN GETZ ESSENTIALS**
00843193 .... $15.99

133. **STAN GETZ FAVORITES**
00843194 .... $15.99

134. **NURSERY RHYMES***
00843196 .... $17.99

135. **JEFF BECK**
00843197 .... $15.99

136. **NAT ADDERLEY**
00843198 .... $15.99

137. **WES MONTGOMERY**
00843199 .... $15.99

138. **FREDDIE HUBBARD**
00843200 .... $15.99

139. **JULIAN "CANNONBALL" ADDERLEY**
00843201 .... $15.99

140. **JOE ZAWINUL**
00843202 .... $15.99

141. **BILL EVANS STANDARDS**
00843156 .... $15.99

142. **CHARLIE PARKER GEMS**
00843222 .... $15.99

143. **JUST THE BLUES**
00843223 .... $15.99

144. **LEE MORGAN**
00843229 .... $15.99

145. **COUNTRY STANDARDS**
00843230 .... $15.99

146. **RAMSEY LEWIS**
00843231 .... $15.99

147. **SAMBA**
00843232 .... $15.99

150. **JAZZ IMPROV BASICS**
00843195 .... $19.99

151. **MODERN JAZZ QUARTET CLASSICS**
00843209 .... $15.99

152. **J.J. JOHNSON**
00843210 .... $15.99

154. **HENRY MANCINI**
00843213 .... $14.99

155. **SMOOTH JAZZ CLASSICS**
00843215 .... $15.99

156. **THELONIOUS MONK – EARLY GEMS**
00843216 .... $15.99

157. **HYMNS**
00843217 .... $15.99

158. **JAZZ COVERS ROCK**
00843219 .... $15.99

159. **MOZART**
00843220 .... $15.99

160. **GEORGE SHEARING**
14041531 .... $16.99

161. **DAVE BRUBECK**
14041556 .... $16.99

162. **BIG CHRISTMAS COLLECTION**
00843221 .... $24.99

164. **HERB ALPERT**
14041775 .... $16.99

165. **GEORGE BENSON**
00843240 .... $16.99

168. **TADD DAMERON**
00103663 .... $15.99

169. **BEST JAZZ STANDARDS**
00109249 .... $19.99

***These CDs do not include split tracks.

0413

Jazz Instruction & Improvisation

BOOKS FOR ALL INSTRUMENTS FROM HAL LEONARD

AN APPROACH TO JAZZ IMPROVISATION
by Dave Pozzi
Musicians Institute Press
Explore the styles of Charlie Parker, Sonny Rollins, Bud Powell and others with this comprehensive guide to jazz improvisation. Covers: scale choices • chord analysis • phrasing • melodies • harmonic progressions • more.
00695135 Book/CD Pack..$17.95

THE ART OF MODULATING
FOR PIANISTS AND JAZZ MUSICIANS
by Carlos Salzedo &
Lucile Lawrence
Schirmer
The Art of Modulating is a treatise originally intended for the harp, but this edition has been edited for use by intermediate keyboardists and other musicians who have an understanding of basic music theory. In its pages you will find: table of intervals; modulation rules; modulation formulas; examples of modulation; extensions and cadences; ten fragments of dances; five characteristic pieces; and more.
50490581 ....$19.99

BUILDING A JAZZ VOCABULARY
By Mike Steinel
A valuable resource for learning the basics of jazz from Mike Steinel of the University of North Texas. It covers: the basics of jazz • how to build effective solos • a comprehensive practice routine • and a jazz vocabulary of the masters.
00849911 ....$19.95

THE CYCLE OF FIFTHS
by Emile and Laura De Cosmo
This essential instruction book provides more than 450 exercises, including hundreds of melodic and rhythmic ideas. The book is designed to help improvisors master the cycle of fifths, one of the primary progressions in music. Guaranteed to refine technique, enhance improvisational fluency, and improve sight-reading!
00311114 ....$16.99

THE DIATONIC CYCLE
by Emile and Laura De Cosmo
Renowned jazz educators Emile and Laura De Cosmo provide more than 300 exercises to help improvisors tackle one of music's most common progressions: the diatonic cycle. This book is guaranteed to refine technique, enhance improvisational fluency, and improve sight-reading!
00311115 ....$16.95

EAR TRAINING
by Keith Wyatt,
Carl Schroeder and Joe Elliott
Musicians Institute Press
Covers: basic pitch matching • singing major and minor scales • identifying intervals • transcribing melodies and rhythm • identifying chords and progressions • seventh chords and the blues • modal interchange, chromaticism, modulation • and more.
00695198 Book/2-CD Pack $24.95

EXERCISES AND ETUDES FOR THE JAZZ INSTRUMENTALIST
by J.J. Johnson
Designed as study material and playable by any instrument, these pieces run the gamut of the jazz experience, featuring common and uncommon time signatures and keys, and styles from ballads to funk. They are progressively graded so that both beginners and professionals will be challenged by the demands of this wonderful music.
00842018 Bass Clef Edition $16.95
00842042 Treble Clef Edition $16.95

JAZZOLOGY
THE ENCYCLOPEDIA OF JAZZ THEORY FOR ALL MUSICIANS
by Robert Rawlins and
Nor Eddine Bahha
This comprehensive resource covers a variety of jazz topics, for beginners and pros of any instrument. The book serves as an encyclopedia for reference, a thorough methodology for the student, and a workbook for the classroom.
00311167 ....$19.99

JAZZ THEORY RESOURCES
by Bert Ligon
Houston Publishing, Inc.
This is a jazz theory text in two volumes. **Volume 1 includes**: review of basic theory • rhythm in jazz performance • triadic generalization • diatonic harmonic progressions and analysis • substitutions and turnarounds • and more. **Volume 2 includes**: modes and modal frameworks • quartal harmony • extended tertian structures and triadic superimposition • pentatonic applications • coloring "outside" the lines and beyond • and more.
00030458 Volume 1 ....$39.95
00030459 Volume 2 ....$29.95

JOY OF IMPROV
by Dave Frank
and John Amaral
This book/CD course on improvisation for all instruments and all styles will help players develop monster musical skills! Book One imparts a solid basis in technique, rhythm, chord theory, ear training and improv concepts. **Book Two** explores more advanced chord voicings, chord arranging techniques and more challenging blues and melodic lines. The CD can be used as a listening and play-along tool.
00220005 Book 1 – Book/CD Pack......................$27.99
00220006 Book 2 – Book/CD Pack......................$26.99

THE PATH TO JAZZ IMPROVISATION
by Emile and Laura De Cosmo
This fascinating jazz instruction book offers an innovative, scholarly approach to the art of improvisation. It includes in-depth analysis and lessons about: cycle of fifths • diatonic cycle • overtone series • pentatonic scale • harmonic and melodic minor scale • polytonal order of keys • blues and bebop scales • modes • and more.
00310904 ....$14.99

THE SOURCE
THE DICTIONARY OF CONTEMPORARY AND TRADITIONAL SCALES
by Steve Barta
This book serves as an informative guide for people who are looking for good, solid information regarding scales, chords, and how they work together. It provides right and left hand fingerings for scales, chords, and complete inversions. Includes over 20 different scales, each written in all 12 keys.
00240885 ....$18.99

21 BEBOP EXERCISES
by Steve Rawlins
This book/CD pack is both a warm-up collection and a manual for bebop phrasing. Its tasty and sophisticated exercises will help you develop your proficiency with jazz interpretation. It concentrates on practice in all twelve keys – moving higher by half-step – to help develop dexterity and range. The companion CD includes all of the exercises in 12 keys.
00315341 Book/CD Pack....................................$17.95

HAL•LEONARD® CORPORATION
7777 W. BLUEMOUND RD. P.O. BOX 13819 MILWAUKEE, WI 53213

Visit Hal Leonard online at
www.halleonard.com

Prices, contents & availability
subject to change without notice.

0113